DATE DUE

TOTALLY GROSS HISTORY™

THE TOTALLY GROSS HISTORY OF ANCIENT ROME

JEREMY KLAR

rosen publishing's rosen central

Published in 2016 by The Rosen Publishing Group, Inc.
29 East 21st Street, New York, NY 10010

First Edition

Library of Congress Cataloging-in-Publication Data

Names: Klar, Jeremy.
Title: The totally gross history of ancient Rome / Jeremy Klar.
Description: First edition. | New York : Rosen Central, 2016. | Series: Totally gross history | Includes bibliographical references and index.
Identifiers: LCCN 2015033911 | ISBN 978-1-4994-3746-1 (library bound) | ISBN 978-1-4994-3744-7 (pbk.) | ISBN 978-1-4994-3745-4 (6-pack)
Subjects: LCSH: Rome—Civilization—Juvenile literature. | Rome—Social life and customs—Juvenile literature.
Classification: LCC DG77 .K57 2016 | DDC 937—dc23
LC record available at http://lccn.loc.gov/2015033911

Manufactured in the United States of America

On the cover: Today visitors to Rome can wander through the extensive ruins of the Roman Forum. The forum was the center of public life in ancient Rome. Many important government buildings and temples were located there.

CONTENTS

INTRODUCTION

The year is 80 CE. You're living in ancient Rome. Today's a special day. You're about to head out to see a show at the circus. As you wind your way through houses, shops, and plazas, you can feel the excitement build up. You reach the circus and take your seat. You're excited for the show to begin. Circuses in ancient Rome were huge open-air theaters, and the shows put on there were full-day affairs. At a circus today, we expect dressed-up elephants and tigers leaping through rings of fire. At a circus in ancient Rome, you watch these same animals march center arena. But instead of animal tricks, suddenly spears fly. You and the rest of the crowd hoot as a team of professional hunters hunt and kill the animals before your very eyes. Animals screech, and blood floods the circus. This probably sounds pretty gruesome to watch. However, for ancient Romans, this bloody show was just a day at the circus.

Many ancient cultures had a different sense of what was disgusting than we do today. A lot of their day-to-day life would certainly gross out a person living today. Between their cleaning habits, the food they ate, and the medicines they used, there was plenty disgusting about life in ancient Rome. The scene of a criminal being clawed at by vicious lions or bears is just one of the brutal spectacles put on in ancient Rome. Realistic battle reenactments (in which people could actually die!), gladiator fights, and other forms of public killings were normal. And the roaring crowds certainly didn't seem to mind all the gore. In fact, it thrilled them.

In this detail from a fourth century CE mosaic, a gladiator spears a bull. Staged animal hunts were a popular, and bloody, form of public entertainment in ancient Rome.

There are plenty of reasons why ancient Romans enjoyed entertainment that we find gross today. Remember, in ancient times they didn't have movies, television, or the printing press. Some of the things we watch at the movie theater today are certainly gory. The difference is that our gore is fake—made in a Hollywood studio with trained actors, makeup, and props. In Roman times, they used real violence to entertain themselves.

Another reason for some of the grosser habits of the ancient Romans is that science couldn't yet explain why some foods or medicines weren't the safest. Without modern science, the Romans didn't know that some of their gross medical concoctions wouldn't really cure disease. They had to rely on crude surgery techniques because there were no better options. Science couldn't explain how to do things better, so practices were basic—and, at times, grueling.

Lastly, we should keep in mind that some things that gross us out aren't really that gross. They're simply different than what we're used to. Some of the weird animals or foods that ancient Romans ate are actually tasty, and many are still popular in other parts of the world. Have you ever traveled to another country with your family and saw something yucky on the menu? Cultural differences are everywhere, and while they may gross us out, they aren't unhealthy or unclean.

With this in mind, let's start our tour of all the totally gross things the ancient Romans used to do. There are a lot of curious facts to learn and some stories that might make you feel queasy. But if you can keep down your lunch, then let's get gross and gruesome.

CHAPTER ONE

TOTALLY GROSS HYGIENE

Many basic ideas of hygiene in ancient Rome were similar to those we have today. After all, the human body worked the same then as it does now. Hygiene includes the basic things we do to stay clean. People in ancient times also needed to use the restroom. They got sweaty and smelled bad, so they needed to bathe. The basic human needs we have today existed. What was different—and often really yucky—was the ways the Romans handled their hygiene.

LONELY ON THE LOO?

Clean, private bathrooms are a major convenience of modern life. Most of us are used to living in areas with plumbing. We have bathrooms at home with a toilet and a sink. At the flush of a button, all the icky stuff that comes out of us disappears into the sewers. Another handle gives us fresh, clean water to wash our hands in seconds. Most bathrooms today also have fans to get rid of the nasty smells. Even public restrooms have stalls for privacy. But in ancient Rome, this wasn't the case.

In Rome, city-goers were never too far from a public latrine, or bathroom. But boy, were they public! In public bathrooms, group toilets were set up around the outside walls of a large, open-air

Roman citizens were never far from public latrines, or bathrooms, where visitors sat on benches and took care of their business—in plain view of everyone else!

room. A stop in the bathroom was a social affair. Some public latrines even had enough spots for up to eighty people to go to the bathroom at the same time! The way these public toilets were laid out meant that every visitor was in full view while doing his or her business. But this didn't bother the Romans. In fact, they often spoke to each other and socialized while they used the latrine.

In one regard, the Romans were quite advanced with their bathrooms. Underneath the long benches that lined their restrooms ran a stream of water. This constantly moving water immediately whisked off any feces into the Roman sewers. This sewage system was a precursor to the modern idea of plumbing.

As advanced as their plumbing was, the Romans did not have the modern luxury of toilet paper that we know so well. In a special documentary for the Smithsonian Channel website, historian and professor Gregory S. Aldrete explains that ancient Romans wiped with "a sponge that was stuck on the end of a stick." These sponge-sticks, called *tersoria*, were shared. Yes, several people wiped themselves using the same sponge, repeatedly rinsed and handed over to the next person! They did use a bucket of water mixed with either vinegar or salt to clean the *tersoria*, but disease spread nonetheless. So next time you rip a square of paper instead of reaching for the family sponge, appreciate the toilet paper.

URINE: THE ULTIMATE DETERGENT BOOSTER

Today, we understand the science of soap. Without going too in depth, we know that the cell-like parts that make up soap attract and trap oil and dirt. Rinsing off the soap carries this dirt and oil away from our body with it. This is how laundry soap works, too. The ancient Romans knew about soap from other cultures, but didn't use it themselves. Instead of soap, they used other kinds of alkali to take the dirt off their clothes.

An alkali is a base that dissolves in water. It works the same way as the soaps or laundry detergents that are household items today. However, the Romans alkali of choice was… urine! Yes, the same waste we flush down the toilets, the Romans collected to clean laundry. Roman clothes were made up of natural fibers, with wool the most common material for tunics and togas. On a hot summer day, boy could wool make a Roman sweat!

The Romans relied on people called *fullones* to clean their clothes (much like a Laundromat or dry cleaner would today). Fullers were highly valued for the dirty job they did. In order to collect enough pee (a whole lot of it was needed to wash a single piece of clothing), fullers left vessels or jars on street corners, outside shops, and near public bathrooms. This urine was so valuable that Emperor Vespasian (who ruled from 69 to 79 CE) created the *vectigal urinae*, or urine tax. The famous Roman author Pliny the Elder even wrote, "Our authorities attribute to urine also great power, not only natural but supernatural."

Once the fullers had collected the urine, they would mix it with water. They would then heat this mixture up in a large tub. The clothes would soak in the mixture. Next, the workers would

In this first century CE fresco, fullers are seen cleaning clothes by stomping all over them while they are soaked in water and urine.

step in and stomp all over the urine-soaked garment with their bare feet. This sounds gross, but all the rough stomping helped break up the dirt and oils staining the clothing. Once sufficiently drenched in pee, the clothes were rinsed with water and hung to dry. It sounds gross, but this clever process was a totally effective way to clean clothes.

HOW ABOUT A GROUP BATH?

Another major element of hygiene in ancient Rome was bathing. Just as with relieving themselves, the Romans turned bathing into a social affair. Bathhouses (*thermae*) were an important spot for communal gathering. The *thermae* each had a series of chambers,

A PRIMARY SOURCE PEEK INTO ROMAN BATHS

Much of what we know about daily life in ancient Rome comes from texts written by Roman authors. While artifacts and archaeological sites give us clues as to how people behaved in ancient times, these primary sources help reveal truly gross stories about Roman practices. A primary source is a first-hand account written by somebody who directly witnessed the events being narrated. Primary sources are particularly useful because their author actually saw what happened. (Nevertheless, a smart reader should always keep in mind that even firsthand witnesses like to embellish, or add exciting details that aren't necessarily true, to make their stories more thrilling.)

One mention of the Roman baths comes from Emperor Marcus Aurelius (who ruled from 161 to 180 CE). In Book 8 of his *Meditations*, the emperor calls bathing "disgusting." He writes, "Such as bathing appears to thee—oil, sweat, dirt, filthy water, all things disgusting—so is every part of life and everything."

Another source that addresses the grossness of the bathhouses is Aulus Cornelius Celsus's book on medicine, *De Medicina*. While giving advice to patients with wounds, Celsus states, "Bathing, too, while the wound is not yet clean, is one of the worst things to do; for this makes the wound both wet and dirty, and then there is a tendency for gangrene to occur." This shows that the Romans had some idea of what caused gangrene—a sickness in which a body part doesn't get enough blood because of infection and the cells die.

or rooms. Each chamber served a different purpose. First was the *apodyterium*, where bathers would undress. The *apodyterium* was like a modern locker room. In it, there were cubbies or shelves to store one's clothes and anything else a bather might be carrying. Slaves kept watch over these belongings while the owners bathed.

This illustration shows the Romans' ingenious method for creating warm pools in their public bathhouses. The pools were a hotbed for bacteria!

The next room was the *palaestra*, or gymnasium. There, Romans could wrestle, exercise, and work up a sweat. We already learned that Romans didn't produce their own soap. So how did they clean themselves in the baths? Before exercising, Romans would apply oils to their skins. These oils mixed with the sweat and dirt on bathers' skin while they exercised.

Unbelievably, getting covered in sweat and dirt isn't the gross part. After the *palaestra* came a series of pools. First was the *frigidarium*, a cold-water pool. Then came the *tepidarium*, or warm pool. Finally, bathers went to the *caldarium*, or steam room. Each of these pools hosted everybody at the same time. Don't forget that all these bathers were naked and had just exercised. With all that built-up oil, dirt, and sweat, everybody took a group bath.

The whole bathing process was a recipe for germs and bacteria—especially in the warm water pools! The water in the bathhouses was not cleaned very often, so all the oil and excrement bathers washed off their bodies stayed in the warm pools.

The final revolting part of the bathing process was when bathers would remove the leftover oil and dirt from their skin. They did this with a metal tool called a strigil. Wealthier Romans had their slaves scrape the oil off for them.

One anecdote shared in the *Augustan History*, a late Roman collection of biographies of the emperors, tells how Emperor Hadrian (who ruled from 117 to 138 CE) once lent one of his slaves to a war veteran after he saw the veteran removing dirt by "rubbing his back and the rest of his body against the wall." Later on the book explains that, in the absence of slaves, bathers had to help clean the oil off each other's bodies.

Shown here is a strigil and flask. The strigil's curved blade was used to scrape off dirt and oil left on the skin after bathing.

CHAPTER TWO

TOTALLY GROSS ENTERTAINMENT

Entertainment was another central part of life in ancient Rome. The Romans loved a good spectacle! But as we already noticed, a lot of what entertained the Romans was violent or bizarre. The primary form of entertainment was the *ludi*, or public games. These games were all-day affairs that served two purposes.

On the one hand, the *ludi* amused the Romans. At the same time, they were performed to please the gods. Before the Roman Empire became Christian, ancient Romans believed in a religion with many different gods who they thought oversaw different parts of life. The Romans offered sacrifices to appease these gods. The *ludi* weren't all fun and games. They were also a major ritual. They took place in amphitheaters and had a variety of activities.

This relief shows the Roman *ludi*, or public games, in action at the Circus Maximus, ancient Rome's largest circus.

ON THE HUNT!

One of the most popular games in the *ludi* was one called the *venatio*.

Venatio is the Latin word for animal hunting. But this wasn't the kind of bird or deer hunting that happens in the woods today. Nowadays, most people who hunt go into the animals' environment. The excitement comes from catching the animal where it can easily hide or escape.

In the Roman *venatio*, exotic animals were brought in to Rome from faraway conquered parts of the empire. Romans built fake woods in the amphitheater especially for these spectacles. There, the animals were turned loose. As a cheering public jeered, trained hunters tracked and killed these wild animals in the arena.

The practice of killing animals from conquered lands started in 251 BCE. That year, elephants were captured from the Carthaginians in a battle in Sicily. The following year, the captive elephants were brought to Rome. Pliny the Elder records the following:

> *There were 142 [elephants], or by some accounts 140, and they had been brought over on rafts that [pontiff] Metellus constructed by laying decks on rows of casks lashed together. Verrius records that [the elephants] fought in the Circus and were killed with javelins, because it was not known what use to make of them, as it had been decided not to keep them nor to present them to native kings.*

Soon, elephants became standard circus fare. Pliny goes on to share a later story of one elephant that was paired off with a prisoner. The prisoner was promised his freedom if he killed the

Romans first encountered elephants during the Punic Wars, in which the Carthaginians brought elephants to the Italian peninsula. The Romans captured the beasts and brought them to Rome to be displayed and killed.

beast. Stories such as this one are common. Keep in mind, people in the Italian peninsula were so unfamiliar with elephants that they called them "oxen," thinking the two animals were related.

In 186 BCE, a special set of religious games took place. A Roman consul named Fulvius promised the gods a ten-day series of games in exchange for a Roman victory in the Aetolian War. In his *History of Rome*, Roman historian Livy notes that, on that occasion, "The hunting of lions and panthers formed a novel [or new] feature."

Over time, emperors introduced even more exotic beasts to the circus. These included crocodiles, snakes, leopards, giraffes,

TO THE LIONS!

While some of the hunting games performed at the circus sound cruel to animals, the Romans didn't treat their human performers any better. One particularly gruesome type of show was the *damnatio ad bestias*. Loosely translated, that's Latin for "death by beasts."

Damnatio ad bestias was a type of punishment for criminals. Just as the *ludi* served a religious purpose and also entertained crowds, "death by beasts" was an "entertaining" way to punish criminals. This form of killing criminals started in the second century BCE and was borrowed from nearby cultures. Criminals were either tied to columns or thrown to animals. They usually had no way to defend themselves. The most popular animal was the lion. Lions were brought in from North Africa specifically for this type of show. This type of sentence both punished the criminal and scared the audience so that they wouldn't commit any crimes either. (It took care of feeding the circus animals, too!)

By the first century CE, *damnatio ad bestias* became a common way of punishing Christians. At first, Romans treated Christians poorly. Christianity was a new religion and a threat to Roman power. Sentenced Christians would be wrapped up in animal skins and then thrown to wild dogs. (In a similar punishment, criminals were wrapped in a *tunica molesta*, a shirt drenched in flammable substances, then publicly set on fire.) By the fourth century, this practice mostly ended since the Roman government began to accept Christianity.

hippopotamuses, and rhinoceroses. The emperors were able to request these exotic animals because the Roman Empire held influence over a large region. Roman armies fought throughout modern-day Europe, North Africa, and the Middle East. Roman historians detailed all the strange animals brought back and slaughtered before amazed Roman eyes.

FIGHT TO THE FINISH: ROMAN GLADIATORS

Gladiators were central figures in ancient Roman entertainment. Days at the amphitheater often wrapped up with gladiator fights. While today's big-buck Hollywood movies make the gladiators seem glamorous and important, this wasn't actually the case.

It is thought that gladiator fights had their origins in old rituals borrowed from the Etruscans (the people who lived in central Italy before the rise of ancient Rome) or the Campanians (who lived just south of Rome). Gladiator fights had their roots in games that were held to honor the dead. Over time, they became a way for powerful people to show off their wealth and influence. In 65 BCE, 320 pairs of gladiators participated in the games that Julius Caesar (who held the public office of *curule aedile*) held in memory of his father. After the Roman Republic gave way to the Roman Empire in the first century CE, the games became a symbol of the power of the state itself. They often reenacted historical fights between Romans and conquered peoples.

Notably, gladiators weren't celebrities in ancient Rome. They were usually captives, slaves, or condemned criminals. Participation in a gladiator fight was a punishment. Foreign soldiers who were captured alive lived on borrowed time. The Romans believed these enemies needed to die to redeem themselves. They were trained and prepared for one last battle.

Musicians accompanied the fights and blasted their trumpets to match particularly dangerous strikes. If the match was a close call, the emperor—or sometimes the audience itself—decided

In this fourth century CE mosaic, gladiators are shown fighting to the death. A far cry from the glamorized heros in Hollywood films, gladiators were typically slaves or criminals sentenced to die.

whether or not the loser should be killed. The public went wild as the condemned fighter took his last breath. Few gladiators survived for longer than ten matches. Death was assured for these fighters.

With the popularity of the fights, however, it became increasingly common to spare gladiators' lives. Costs, however, made it difficult to fulfill public demand. In 325 CE, Emperor Constantine I (who ruled from 306 to 337 CE) banned gladiatorial games for good.

SIMULATING THE HIGH SEAS

One of the most over-the-top forms of entertainment in Ancient Rome was a type of staged naval battle called a *naumachia*. The *naumachiae* (plural of *naumachia*) were originally held in large man-made lakes. Prisoners who were sentenced to death were forced to recreate historical naval battles. The recreations only ended when one team won and the other was dead. Because of the number of participants—and the fact that these reenactments always ended in death—*naumachiae* were much bloodier (and grosser to watch) than the gladiator fights.

The first *naumachia* occurred in 46 BCE and was sponsored by Julius Caesar. It celebrated his recent military victories in Gaul and Egypt. For the celebration, Caesar had a giant basin dug near the Tiber River, which runs through Rome. This basin was filled with water. Four thousand rowers and one thousand men fought on each side in this *naumachia*.

In the year 2 BCE, Augustus (who ruled from 27 BCE to 14 CE) staged another *naumachia*, recreating a historic Greek naval

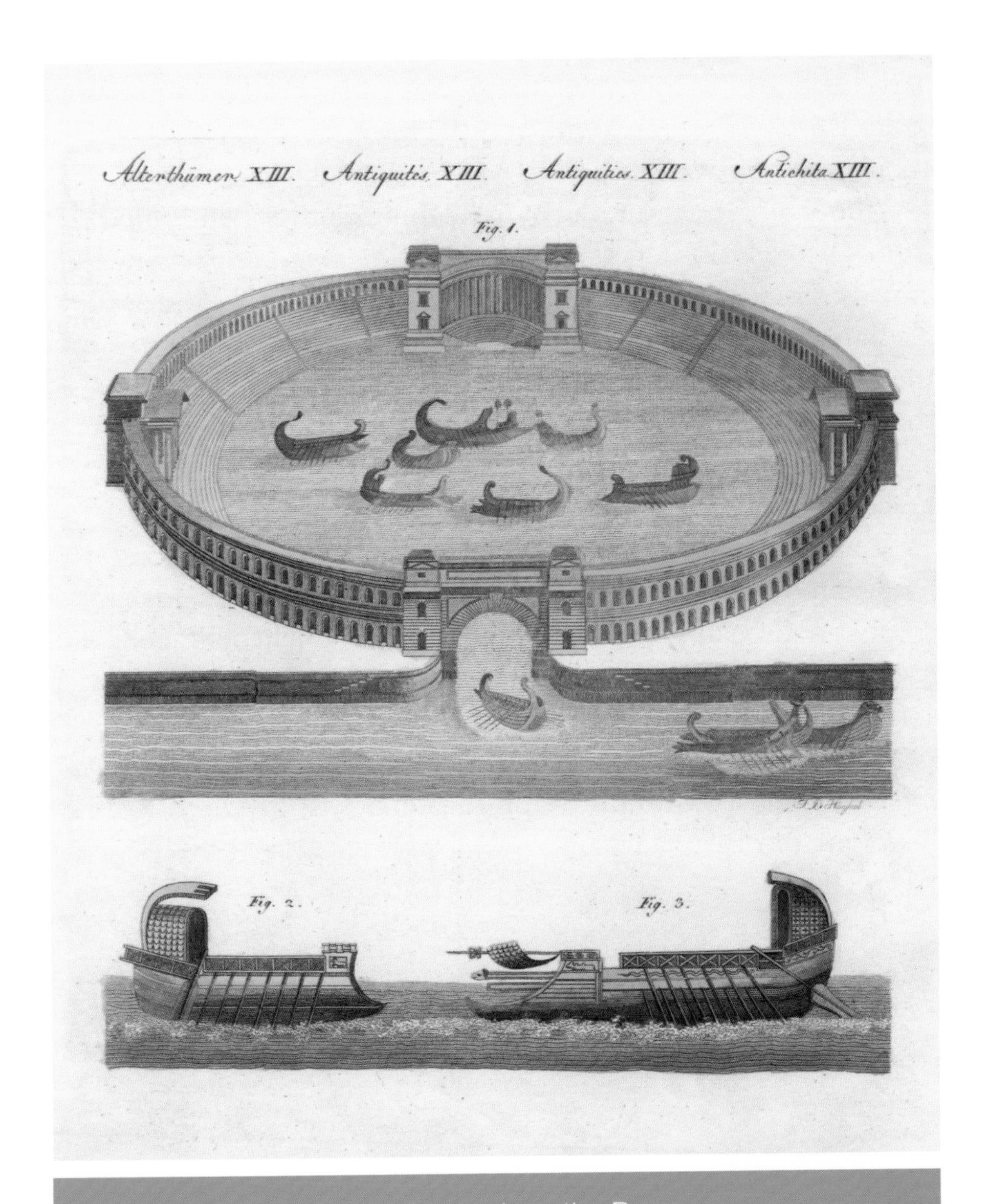

This colored engraving depicts how the Roman *naumachiae* would have appeared. Spectators watched as naval reenactments left the amphitheater lake red with blood.

battle at Salamis. This mock battle was carried out on a massive scale. Thirty ships were used, and the basin held over 270,000 cubic meters of water!

About a half-century later, in 52 CE, Claudius (who ruled from 41 to 54 CE) staged another grand *naumachia.* To wow the crowds, Claudius's show featured one hundred ships and 19,000 gladiators. Roman bodyguards surrounded the fake lake to stop the participants from escaping. The Roman public cheered as the participants fought to the death. Claudius did spare many of the gladiators but only after the water had turned red with much blood.

Because the *naumachiae* involved so many ships (making it hard to move around), they often involved more hand-to-hand combat than major boat attacks. Prisoners punched, lunged, and used the weapons they were given to slaughter each other center stage. The events were truly gruesome.

Under Emperor Nero (who ruled from 54 to 68 CE), *naumachiae* were moved into the amphitheaters. Cassius Dio, a Roman historian, records:

> *In the course of producing a spectacle at one of the theatres, [Nero] suddenly filled the place with sea water so that fishes and sea monsters swam about in it, and he exhibited a naval battle between men representing Persians and Athenians.*

When the *naumachia* was complete, "he immediately drew off the water, dried the ground, and once more exhibited contests between land forces."

Of course, the cost of producing these shows and the major use of water made them impractical. By the fifth century CE, the *naumachiae* had mostly ended. Their legacy, however, continued to inspire others for centuries to come. King Henry II of France held one in 1550, and Napoleon held another in 1807. In eighteenth-century England, mock naval battles using toy ships became a popular park activity.

Romans took their entertainment pretty seriously. And more often than not, it was a life-or-death matter. Whether it involved humans killing animals, animals killing humans, or humans forced to kill each other, a Roman show always involved a lot of spilled blood.

CHAPTER THREE

TOTALLY GROSS DIET

In the realm of totally gross stuff, food is something really up to a person's taste. In every culture, there are certain dishes that some people love and others find gross. And while tastes for food vary among people living in the same place, they're especially different from culture to culture. This is because we learn to like or dislike a lot of foods from the culture we grow up in.

The ancient Romans ate a lot of the foods we eat today, but they also had some strange dishes that would turn a modern diner's stomach. Little rodents called dormice were a delicacy. The Romans even fattened them up before slaughtering them for dinner.

Many of the grossest ancient Roman recipes that we know of today come from a text called *Apicius*. This ancient Roman cookbook was named after the ancient Roman gourmet Marcus Gavius Apicius. (While the book was written during the fourth or fifth century CE, Apicius lived around 90 BCE.)

A BIRD ON THE PLATE IS WORTH TWO IN THE BUSH

Poultry—birds that are raised to be eaten, such as chicken or turkey—has featured in human diets for most of recorded history. Poultry is a good source of protein in a diet. It is also considered edible in most religious diets. Romans ate many of the same birds that we eat today, including chicken and geese. However, they also ate a few birds that would make readers today cringe a little.

One popular Roman choice was the thrush. The thrush is a small songbird that, in Roman markets, fetched a high value for its flavor. The Roman poet Horace wrote that, "Nothing is more delicious than thrushes," while the poet Martial claimed that, "the thrush is the greatest delicacy among birds." Today, eating

This ancient Roman mosaic depicts a cockfight. Romans ate many of the same birds we do today, but prepared in strange ways, in addition to a few other birds we wouldn't dare touch.

thrushes is widely looked down upon. In fact, killing thrushes for food is banned in the European Union.

Other songbirds (*beccaficoes*) were popular sources of meat as well. The *ficedula*, or figpecker, was another popular protein. These songbirds were small, yet plump, making their meat tender. Nightingales were the most valuable small songbirds. One single nightingale could fetch more money than the cost of a slave! Because of their size, the Romans often didn't bother gutting *beccaficoes* for their meat. They would eat the birds whole. One particularly outrageous recipe—published in *Apicius*—called for a meat pie made entirely of lark tongue. Considering how small larks are, one can only imagine how many of their tongues it took to make one single meat pie.

The Romans kept songbirds in enclosures called aviaries while they fattened them up. They kept the birds in the dark, as they believed this would make the birds less active and they would fatten up more quickly.

Other members of the bird family were often eaten not because of their taste but because of their exotic appearance. Birds such as the peacock and pheasant would be plucked before cooking but then have their feathers stuck back in before being served. Presentation was everything.

Parrots, ibises, ostriches, and flamingos were other exotic delicacies. Parrot brains and flamingo tongues were considered especially fancy, but the entire birds could also be boiled with spices and served that way. Cranes, too, would be boiled and served. Eating these strange birds was a sign of the Roman Empire's far-reaching power.

The Romans enjoyed a variety of exotic birds that were favored for their beautiful or strange appearance. Parrots, flamingos, ibises, and cranes were just a few of the strange dishes Romans served.

CREATURES OF THE SEA

Strange birds weren't the only disgusting things you could find on a Roman dinner table. The Romans also fancied certain deep-sea critters that we wouldn't dare consider tasting. One notable dish was the moray eel, or *murena*. The Romans actually raised the dangerous carnivorous eels in pools, so there was always a ready supply of them. They also feasted on electric eels and conger eels.

As with exotic birds, the presentation of the eels was important. *A Dictionary of Roman and Greek Antiquities*, notes that, "In the banquet of Nasidienus, an eel is brought, garnished with prawns [or shrimp] swimming in the sauce."

Just like the lark tongue meat pie, the *Apicius* cookbook is the source of a few of the most revolting seafood recipes. These dishes involve unusual ocean inhabitants served in a familiar way. Take, for instance, "dolphin balls." As an ocean mammal, dolphin meat was said to be somewhere between beef and tuna in texture. *Apicius*'s recipe calls for skinning the dolphin and cutting its flesh into small rolled balls. These meatballs would be cooked in wine, oil, and a popular fish sauce of the time

Ancient Roman banquets were fancy affairs. Hosts took great pride in serving bizarre foods or preparing common foods in strange ways.

SOMETHING SMELLS FISHY

The Romans had a taste for fish sauces—and they served them with just about everything. The most popular condiment was a fermented sauce called *garum*. It was made from the intestines of mackerel (which is a kind of fish). *Garum* was also common throughout the rest of the Mediterranean region. The process of making it was later described in a tenth-century Greek text, the *Geoponika*:

> *The intestines of fish are thrown into a vessel, and are salted... and they are seasoned in the sun, and frequently turned; and when they have been seasoned in the heat, the garum is thus taken from them.*

After being salted, the mackerel was left in the sun a whopping one to three months!

Another fish sauce, which was cheaper, was called *muria*. It was salty. Because it was cheaper, *muria* was used to pickle or preserve foods. However, the cheapest sauce was *allec*. *Allec* was the sludge left behind from the *garum*-making process—that is, the decomposed fish intestines. Cato the Elder notes that *allec* (which he spelled as *hallec*) was what he fed his slaves if he ran out of other cheap foods.

Gross as these fish sauces sound, the condiments were very healthy. They were packed with proteins, amino acids, minerals, and vitamin B.

Shown are the ruins of an ancient Roman *garum* factory in Setúbal, Portugal. This salty fish paste was the ketchup of the Roman world.

called *garum*. Season and serve. (And keep a bucket nearby in case you truly can't stomach it!)

Fried shark, prepared similarly, was another deep-sea delicacy in some Roman banquets. Stuffed sea urchins—filled with foods such as leaves, pepper, honey, and egg—were also a feature on the menu.

If you aren't already totally queasy, there's one more seafood dish from the *Apicius* cookbook to push you over the edge. It's the jellyfish omelet. In Roman times, jellyfish were commonly served as a salad. However, *Apicius* calls for jellyfish in its *patina de apua sine apua* (which is Latin for "anchovy omelet without anchovies"). If prepared well, the recipe notes, "no one at the table will know what he is eating."

Sound deceptive? The idea of being tricked into eating jellyfish in place of anchovies seems like it would get a restaurant today shut down. However, the Romans saw exotic cuisine as an art form. Successfully preparing a strange dish so that the diners couldn't tell anything was fishy was considered mastery in the kitchen.

In fact, for ancient Romans, grossness seems to be a major ingredient in most recipes. Whether it was an exotic animal or an outlandish presentation, the element of shock excited wealthy diners. Thankfully, health codes today keep surprises out of our dishes.

CHAPTER FOUR

TOTALLY GROSS MEDICINE

As long as humans have been around, people have gotten sick. And when people get sick, they use medicine to get better. Medicine is the branch of science that deals with figuring out how a person is sick and what he or she needs to get better. In ancient times, this could be special plants or foods, prayers, or surgery.

Today, governments test new medicines and make rules for how people can take them. Doctors are specially trained in how to safely perform surgeries. We understand how bacteria and germs are spread. But before modern science existed, many people—the ancient Romans included—relied on folk medicine and simple tools. And some of the ways they "cured" the sick sound, in fact, sickening.

STRANGE REMEDIES

Without a good understanding of how the body works, the Romans often believed in odd treatments. For instance, Pliny the Elder wrote: "The old Romans assigned to wool even supernatural powers… and besides dress and protection from cold, unwashed wool supplies very many remedies if dipped in oil and wine or vinegar."

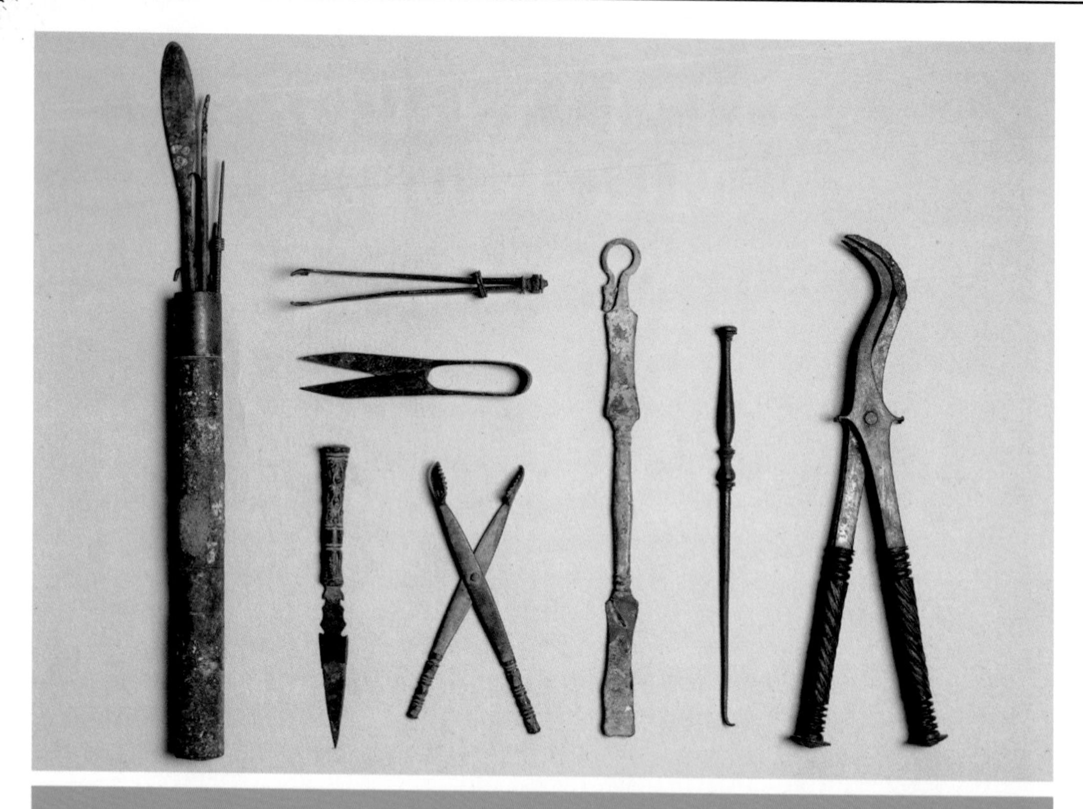

Like many of the folk remedies that Roman physicians prescribed, the tools and techniques used for surgeries were simple, as was the Roman understanding of how the human body worked.

Romans believed that raw sheep wool could heal bruises, swelling, or even open wounds. They also thought that if applied to a woman's private parts after giving birth, unwashed wool could relieve the pain of childbirth.

Raw wool that was especially full of greasy sheep sweat had special uses. Pliny notes that it was applied to the eyes and eyelids to cure redness. It was also thought to cure itching near the private parts. Perhaps most disgusting, Pliny shares, "The sweaty grease too that gathers into pills about the [sheep's] tail, dried by itself and ground to powder, is wonderfully beneficial if rubbed on the teeth." Sweaty sheep wool was thought to heal mouth sores along the gums. Yuck!

Another popular remedy in ancient Rome was cabbage. Cato the Elder recommended cabbage to help with digestion. In fact, Cato couldn't recommend cabbage enough for a variety of stomach problems. However, cabbage had an even better use, according to Cato. In *De Agri Cultura*, he says:

And still further, if you save the urine of a person who eats cabbage habitually, heat it, and bathe the patient in it, he will be healed quickly; this remedy has been tested. Also, if babies are bathed in this urine they will never be weakly; those whose eyes are not very clear will see better if they are bathed in this urine; and pain in the head or neck will be relieved if the heated urine is applied.

However amazing cabbage was thought to be, it was even better to bathe in the urine of somebody else who had eaten it.

Still not convinced of the grossness of Roman medicine? Consider the Roman equivalent of a juice cleanse. Cato recommends a rather sickly concoction.

Cabbage was held in high regard. Unfortunately, consuming cabbage was not as popular a remedy as was bathing in the urine of somebody else who had eaten cabbage. Yuck!

His recipe includes ham, cabbage, beets, fern, fish, a scorpion, six snails, wine, and lentils. Everything was boiled together and then drunk in three parts. This remedy was said to clear out the stomach.

OUT FOR BLOOD

Much of what we know about ancient Roman habits and medicines comes from the writings of Cato the Elder, a Roman senator and historian.

The ancient Romans also had a belief system about how the body worked that science would later debunk. Doctors in ancient Greece and Rome alike thought that the human body held four substances, called "humors." They were yellow bile, black bile, phlegm, and blood. For a patient to be healthy, the four humors needed to be balanced.

In the second century CE, an important Greek doctor living and working in Rome, named Galen of Pergamum, taught that blood was the most common humor. Galen's teachings helped make a practice called bloodletting wildly popular.

Bloodletting involves intentionally cutting a patient to release blood from his or her body. Some techniques involved simple cuts. More advanced techniques involved multiple cuts and the use of suction to draw out extra blood. Galen created a system that explained how releasing blood from different parts of the body could cure different types of disease. The more deadly the disease, the more blood needed to be let.

Of course, medical science has since proven that this theory is not only wrong, but it is also dangerous. Many people have died throughout history because of bloodletting. But in ancient Rome, it was the go-to technique for things as simple as a headache. Galen even created do-it-yourself guide on how to let blood at home.

The obsession with blood didn't stop at cutting a sick patient's body. Another popular belief in Roman medicine was that

This relief depicts a patient having his blood let. Romans (and people from many other civilizations) believed that bloodletting could cure a variety of maladies. Modern science has proved this notion false.

drinking the blood of a gladiator could cure epilepsy. Epilepsy is a brain disorder that causes a person to shake uncontrollably in seizures. Pliny the Elder mentions the practice in his writings ("Epileptic patients are in the habit of drinking the blood even of gladiators"), as does Celsus ("Some have freed themselves from [epilepsy] by drinking the hot blood from the cut throat of a gladiator").

These icky medicines and gross surgeries may sound unbelievable to anybody today. But like most of the disgusting parts

DRILLING FOR PHLEGM

Blood wasn't the only humor that Romans thought was dangerous in excess. Phlegm was also suspected of pooling up in head lesions. The solution? Galen of Pergamum and other doctors of the era believed in a practice called trepanation. Trepanation involves drilling a hole in a patient's head to expose the skull and drain excess fluids. The wounds were designed to stay open and heal slowly. This would allow built-up fluids to drain out. One can just imagine the sick of Rome wandering the streets with open gashes in their skulls.

To carry out trepanation, doctors used a variety of tools. The tools were usually metal. Each one was designed to create a different kind of incision, but the most common was a trepan, which was much like a manual drill. For one procedure, Galen recommended a simple chisel. As gross as the surgery was, a similar surgery called a craniotomy does exist today, although anesthesia and tools have improved greatly. Furthermore, today's patients get the holes in their heads closed up before leaving the hospital.

of life in ancient Rome, cultural differences are to blame. How often do you dislike the taste of a medicine but take it because you think it will make you feel better? Can you remember a time when somebody ordered something at a restaurant that you thought was sickening?

There are plenty of revolting things about life in ancient Rome, but the Romans also made major contributions to the arts, politics, science, and medicine. Elements of their culture have been passed down, and their language (Latin) became the source of Spanish, French, Italian, and all other Romance languages. So before you judge some of their grosser practices, be open-minded and consider the popular saying: "When in Rome, do as the Romans do."

GLOSSARY

appease To make another happy or less angry by giving or doing something he or she wants.

captive Somebody taken prisoner or held against his or her will.

communal Shared by all of the people in a community.

concoction A mixture of different things.

condemned Sentenced to a certain punishment or found guilty.

crude Primitive, simple, or basic.

delicacy A food that is considered rare, exotic, or expensive.

edible Capable of being safely eaten.

exotic Something exciting because of its foreignness.

fuller One who washes or cleans clothes.

hygiene The practices or behaviors that people do in order to stay clean.

latrine A toilet; a hole or receptacle used as a toilet.

precursor Something that comes before something else and leads to it.

reenactment The acting out of a previous action.

ritual A ceremony, especially a religious one, with actions that are carried out in a particular order.

sacrifice A religious ceremony in which a human or animal is killed to please a god.

sentence A punishment given to a guilty person as judgment for his or her crime.

socialize To interact in a social group.

spectacle A show or scene that is entertaining or otherwise captures attention.

FOR MORE INFORMATION

American Institute for Roman Culture (AIRC)
1101 West 34th Street, Suite 730-174
Austin, TX 78705
(512) 772-1844
Website: http://www.romanculture.org
The AIRC is dedicated to promoting the study of Roman culture through study abroad programs, excavation work, and preservation initiatives.

Archaeological Institute of America (AIA)
Boston University
656 Beacon Street, 6th Floor
Boston, MA 02215
(617) 353-9361
Website: http://www.archaeological.org
The AIA is a nonprofit organization dedicated to preventing the destruction of archaeological sites, exploring how archaeology helps us understand the past and future, and increasing public interest in archaeology.

British Museum
Department of Greece and Rome
Great Russell Street
London
WC1B 3DG
United Kingdom
+44 (0) 20 7323 8321
Website: http://www.britishmuseum.org/about_us/departments/greece_and_rome.aspx

The British Museum is one of the world's most respected institutions. Formed in 1860, the Department of Greek and Roman Antiquities holds over 100,000 objects dating back to 3,000 BCE.

Metropolitan Museum of Art
1000 Fifth Avenue
New York, NY 10028
(212) 535-7710
Website: http://www.metmuseum.org
New York City's Metropolitan Museum of Art has an extensive collection of over 17,000 ancient Roman and Greek works of art and artifacts. Its Department of Greek and Roman Art also actively publishes research and carries out scholarly archaeological fieldwork.

Montreal Museum of Fine Arts (MMFA)
P.O. Box 3000, Station "H"
Montreal, Quebec H3G 2T9
Canada
(514) 285-2000
(800) 899-MUSE
Website: http://www.mbam.qc.ca/en
Founded in 1860, the MMFA's World Cultures and Mediterranean Archaeology collections hold an unparalleled 9,640 objects—one of the largest holdings in Canada. Sculptures, reliefs, ceramics, and other artifacts shed light on ancient civilizations, including ancient Rome.

National Junior Classical League (NJCL)
860 NW Washington Boulevard, Suite A
Hamilton, OH 45013
(513) 529-7741
Website: http://www.njcl.org
Established in 1936, the NJCL encourages middle and high school students to take an active interest in the arts, language, literature, and culture of ancient Greece and Rome.

Royal Ontario Museum (ROM)
100 Queen's Park
Toronto, ON M5S 2C6
Canada
(416) 586-8000
Website: http://www.rom.on.ca/en
ROM Ancient Cultures is the museum's center of discovery dedicated to excavating, studying, and preserving artifacts from ancient civilizations, including ancient Rome.

WEBSITES

Because of the changing nature of Internet links, Rosen Publishing has developed an online list of websites related to the subject of this book. This site is updated regularly. Please use this link to access this list:

http://www.rosenlinks.com/TGH/Rome

FOR FURTHER READING

Allen, Kathy. *Disgusting History: The Smelliest, Dirtiest Eras of the Past 10,000 Years*. North Mankato, MN: Capstone Press, 2014.

Botham, Noel & Chris Mitchell. *Did Romans Really Wash Themselves In Wee? And Other Freaky, Funny and Horrible History Facts*. New York, NY: John Blake Publishing, 2014.

Corrick, James A. *The Bloody, Rotten Roman Empire: The Disgusting Details about Life in Ancient Rome*. North Mankato, MN: Capstone Press, 2011.

Crompton, Samuel Willard. *Discovering Ancient Rome* (Exploring Ancient Civilizations). New York, NY: Britannica Educational Publishing, 2015.

England, Victoria & David Antram. *Top 10 Worst Things about Ancient Rome: You Wouldn't Want to Know!* New York, NY: Gareth Stevens, 2012.

Gifford, Clive & Paul Cherrill. *Food and Cooking in Ancient Rome*. New York, NY: PowerKids Press, 2010.

Hamen, Susan E. *Ancient Rome* (Ancient Civilizations). North Mankato, MN: Essential Library, 2015.

Hardyman, Robyn. *Horrible Jobs in Ancient Greece and Rome*. New York, NY: Gareth Stevens, 2014.

Holm, Kirsten C. *Everyday Life in Ancient Rome*. New York, NY: PowerKids Press, 2012.

Kops, Deborah. *Discover Ancient Rome* (Discover Ancient Civilizations). Berkeley Heights, NJ: Enslow Publishers, 2014.

Nardo, Don. *Daily Life in Ancient Rome* (Daily Life in Ancient Civilizations). London, England: Raintree, 2015.

Yomtov, Nelson. *The Grimy, Gross Unusual History of the Toilet*. North Mankato, MN: Capstone Press, 2012.

BIBLIOGRAPHY

Aurelius, Marcus. *Meditations.* Translated by George Long. Retrieved June 25, 2015 (http://classics.mit.edu/Antoninus/meditations.html).

"Baths." PBS.org. Retrieved June 25, 2015 (http://www.pbs.org/empires/romans/empire/baths.html).

Cato the Elder. *De Agricultura.* Translated by W. D. Hooper and H. B. Ash. Retrieved August 11, 2015 (http://penelope.uchicago.edu/Thayer/E/Roman/Texts/Cato/De_Agricultura/home.html).

Celsus, Aulus Cornelius. *De Medicina.* Translated and edited by W. G. Spencer. Retrieved June 25, 2015 (http://www.perseus.tufts.edu/hopper/text?doc=Perseus%3atext%3a1999.02.0142).

Curtis, Robert I. "Salted Fish Products in Ancient Medicine." *Journal of the History of Medicine and Allied Sciences*, XXXIX, 4. 1984, pp. 430–445.

Dio, Cassius. *Roman History.* Retrieved July 14, 2015 (http://penelope.uchicago.edu/Thayer/E/Roman/Texts/Cassius_Dio/home.html).

Faas, Patrick. *Around the Roman Table: Food and Feasting in Ancient Rome*. New York, NY: Palgrave MacMillan, 2003.

Greenstone, Gerry. "The History of Bloodletting." *BC Medical Journal*, vol. 52, no. 1. January/February 2010. Retrieved August 11, 2015 (http://www.bcmj.org/premise/history-bloodletting).

Historia Augusta: The Scriptores. Translated by David Magie. London, UK: Heinemann, 1961–67.

Krulwich, Robert. "Who Wants To Eat Jellyfish Omelets? Dolphin Meatballs? Mouse-On-Toast? These Guys." NPR.

September 27, 2012. Retrieved August 10, 2015 (http://www.npr.org/sections/krulwich/2012/09/27/161874316/who-wants-to-eat-jellyfish-omelettes-dolphin-meatballs-mouse-on-toast-these-guys).

Livius, Titus. *History of Rome: Book 39*. Translated by Rev. Canon Roberts. London, UK: J. M. Dent & Sons, Ltd., 1905. Retrieved June 25, 2015 (http://mcadams.posc.mu.edu/txt/ah/Livy/Livy39.html).

Mirsky, Steve. "Toilet Issue: Anthropologists Uncover All the Ways We've Wiped." *Scientific American*, vol. 308, issue 3. Retrieved June 25, 2015 (http://www.scientificamerican.com/article/toilet-tissue-anthropologists-uncover-all-the-ways-weve-wiped/?page=1).

Missios, Symeon. "Hippocrates, Galen, and the Uses of Trepanation in the Ancient Classical World." *Neurosurgical Focus*, vol. 23, no. 1. 2007. Retrieved August 12, 2015 (http://thejns.org/doi/pdf/10.3171/FOC-07/07/E11).

Pliny the Elder. *Natural History*. Cambridge, MA: Harvard University Press, 1949–54. Retrieved June 25, 2015 (http://www.masseiana.org/pliny.htm).

Smith, William, ed. *A Dictionary of Greek and Roman Antiquities*. LacusCurtius: Into the Roman World. Retrieved June 18, 2015 (http://penelope.uchicago.edu/Thayer/E/Roman/Texts/secondary/SMIGRA/home.html).

Smithsonian Channel. "Danger Lurks in a Roman Latrine." Retrieved June 25, 2015 (http://www.smithsonianmag.com/videos/category/science/sharing-toilets-with-friends-and-evil-spirits/?no-ist).

Tschen-Emmons, James B. *Artifacts from Ancient Rome*. Santa Barbara, CA: ABC-CLIO, 2014.

Vester, Christina. "Cleverness, Cleanliness, and Urine in Ancient Rome." *Labyrinth: Classical Studies Department, University of Waterloo*, issue 89 (2009). Retrieved June 25, 2015 (http://www.classics.uwaterloo.ca/labyrinth_old/issue89/Pee.02.09.pdf).

Walker, Harlan. *Fish: Food from the Waters* (Proceedings from the Oxford Symposium on Food and Cookery 1997). Devon, UK: Prospect Books, 1998.

INDEX

ABOUT THE AUTHOR

Jeremy Klar is a writer and history buff. He currently lives in Brooklyn, NY.

PHOTO CREDITS

Cover, p. 1 Phant/Shutterstock.com; p. 5 Galleria Borghese, Rome, Italy/Alinari/Bridgeman Images; p. 8 Joseph Calev/ Shutterstock.com; p. 10 DEA/L. Pedicini/De Agostini/Getty Images; pp. 12, 35 De Agostini Picture Library/Getty Images; p. 13 Heritage Images/Hulton Archive/Getty Images; pp. 14, 25 DEA/A. Dagli Orti/De Agostini/Getty Images; p. 16 © Pictorial Press Ltd/Alamy; pp. 19, 28 DEA/G. Dagli Orti /De Agostini/Getty Images; p. 21 Private Collection/ © Purix Verlag Volker Christen/Bridgeman Images; p. 27 DEA/C. Sappa/ De Agostini/Getty Images; p. 29 © Manuel Ribeiro/Alamy; p. 32 Mondadori Portfolio/Getty Images; p. 33 DigiCake/Shutterstock.com; p. 34 Vatican Museums and Galleries, Vatican City/ Alinari/Bridgeman Images; cover and interior pages Lukiyanova Natalia/frenta/Shutterstock.com (splatters), idea for life/Shutterstock.com, Ensuper/Shutterstock.com, ilolab/Shutterstock.com, Sfio Cracho/Shutterstock.com, Apostrophe/Shutterstock.com (textures and patterns)

Designer: Michael Moy; Editor: Amelie Von Zumbusch; Photo Researcher: Karen Huang